The spiritual journey is individual, highly
personal. It can't be organized or regulated.
It isn't true that everyone should follow
one path. Listen to your own truth.

—Ram Dass

In the process of writing this book, several times the thought of a dedication page would cross my mind.

Where I am very blessed with my family and friends in my life and would gladly dedicate this book to any one of them, that isn't what I feel pulled to do.

I would love to dedicate this book to each and every one of you. Those of you picking up this book to give it a chance and, more importantly, to each of you willing to even take a single step to becoming "One with God." With all the time and energy I spent putting this book together, I feel extremely grateful that you have taken a little time out of your day to embrace the concept of embarking on a spiritual journey together. Even though they will be very personal and different to each of us, we can all arrive to a destination that one could have only dreamed or imagined existed, a place where we will feel a connection with God unlike anything we thought possible. Our own personal chance to be "One with God."

I would like to acknowledge Jimmy Gammon for his contributions to this book. When he agreed to collaborate on this book with me, it gave me confidence to continue on and power through. Where I was extremely excited about the journey, I was a little nervous about my own abilities. Jimmy, my childhood friend, always had a love for writing. I knew he would be the perfect addition to this project. I am extremely grateful for all he added to the book, but I'm even more grateful for our lifelong friendship.

Thank you from the bottom of my heart, and enjoy your journey.

The desire to know your own soul
will end all other desires.

—Rumi

CONTENTS

INTRODUCTION

It is Friday afternoon. Work is done, dishes are clean, and you sink into your favorite chair. Cold drink at arm's length and your favorite snack in your lap, and for the first time all week, you can just breathe. As the tension leaves your body and your mind goes at ease, you look back at your week. Work is going well. Pretty much the same day in and day out, and it pays the rent, the bills, and puts food in the fridge. Your relationship with your partner is strong, and the kids are doing fine. These are the days we should cherish because life is how we always thought it should be; however, you feel as though something is missing. It isn't anything you can put your finger on, but just an emptiness, a void of sorts. Perhaps it is just a feeling that when things are going well, then something is going to happen to change that. Or maybe it's something more. Then your finger pushes the button on the remote, sending a signal to the television, and once again, these worries are erased by the characters on the screen. That hole we were sensing will have to wait for another day.

I propose that you hit that remote button again and let the screen pause or go dark because today is the day that the hole sees light. God did not make us to feel empty, but to be full. I would like for us to take a journey over the next hour or two, a journey that is always present for us but that is often neglected. We are going to unlock and open untapped areas that may have been locked away over time or that perhaps you have never experienced. The journey will be different for each of us, but the ultimate goal is to find that place of peace within ourselves, a place where we can find the wholeness that He has for us. The road may twist and turn, obstacles arise and distractions surface, but each one of us are commissioned to find that inner peace.

On this adventure, you do not need to pack or make detailed plans. We are going to let the path take us where it may. You will not need any money, and you will not need to use any valuable vacation days. The only things you will need is your heart, your imagination, and a complete open mind to the possibilities that lie within you. You may need a little patience also because this is not a "blink and you are there" trip. This is a journey that should be dissected, thought about, and savored. It is a journey to discover our "Oneness with God." In the following chapters, we hope to open your eyes and ears and hearts to all the beauty that exists within you and the world around you. We hope to help you discover how to feel "One with God."

The only temple that matters can
be found within yourself.

—The Dalai Lama

1

THE WAREHOUSE

Let us search out and examine our ways,
and turn back to the Lord; Let us lift our
hearts and hands to God in heaven.

—Lamentations 3:40–41

Our journey will begin as any should—with an evaluation of where we are, where we have been, and where we are going. We will begin in a warehouse that holds and protects the records of our past, present, and future. In other words, the records in our minds and hearts. Our past experiences and interactions have trained this part of our brain to be on "autopilot" to the point that we react, respond, and generally interact before we even consider other responses or the consequences of our words and actions. For the most part, these conditioned responses will probably work out fine as they have served us well in the past.

The purpose of this book is to be more deliberate in our actions and responses in order to enhance and strengthen the impact of what we do and say. Atticus Finch once said, "You never know a man until you stand in his shoes and walk about in them." Wouldn't it be amazing if we would pause and actually put ourselves in the other person's shoes before we respond to them? Doing so could perhaps change their life, and it would definitely change ours.

Now, let's get back to our warehouse for a little exploring. The room is massive and lined with shelves on three sides. So many shelves—shelves on the left, shelves on the right, and shelves dead straight ahead. The shelves are there to do what shelves do: organize and store our junk, our stuff.

The shelves on the left hold everything that you have ever been taught—everything from birth to today. On the far left is our infant stage. We learn that eating stops hunger; the warmth of another person's skin next to ours is comforting; that if we make loud enough sounds, someone will listen and respond; and if we make a mess in our diaper, it is nice to have someone help us clean it up—all of which are true today as adults.

We begin to crawl, walk, and talk. Toys teach us shapes and colors. We learn what textures are, that sweet food taste better than bitter food. We aren't even school age yet, but a picture of the world is evolving. Can you see the shelves on the left getting filled? Then school begins. Wow, there are shelves and shelves of all the years of history, science, math, and English. Oh my gosh! There is calculus and Shakespeare, also books and books we were assigned to read, along with the ones we chose to read. We were taught to play games in gym, how to take turns and share; music, band, dance, sports, shop, and on and on. There was something for everyone who wanted it, and there still is.

Perhaps the most important things we learned in school was how to mingle with people, to interact with peers in so many different ways and settings. So many people to meet. So many different types of people and groups. Where would we fit in? Many of us continue to struggle with that question today. Some people learned how to bully and pick on weaker kids. Some learned how to stand up for those weaker kids. Some learned to try and be invisible. We learned the slightest little thing made us feel different and weird and insecure. Those experiences helped shape us into the people we are today, be it good or bad. Whether we picked or got picked on, it is part of our psyche.

Our learned behaviors have become something that doesn't just affect us but affects the ones around us. The cold, hard truth of the matter is that even if we didn't pick or get picked on, we all knew someone who did. Did we stand up and do the right thing? If not, then we are as culpable as the people who did it.

Unfortunately, the one thing in the world that can never change is the past. Oh, the memory of the facts can be altered and interpretations can vary, but you can't change the truth. Past transgressions may be forgiven or tempered over time, but the pains imposed may always be felt. The fortunate fact is that our past indiscretions do not have to guide our future acts; they do not have to define what we become.

God gave man the ability to reason, process, and think. So we can make excuses, or we can make amends. At times, it may be difficult to look at the person in the mirror, but real change must begin with that person. We may not be able to change the world, but we can work on changing ourselves and the little part of the world around us.

Don't think or believe for a second that the person you are today has to be the person you see tomorrow. We continue to develop this learned behavior even as grown adults. Ask yourself and be honest: when was the last time you let your heart take the lead? Our brains tend to overthink things, make excuses, find reasons to not get involved or to do what is right. When we lead with the heart, we rarely end with regret.

Compassion, empathy, sympathy, caring, love, and so on and so on—these are the tools of the heart—and when we make decisions with the heart as the guide, we begin to change who we are, change others, and change our part in the world. The shelves on the right contain everything you have ever done that was led by the heart. Every act of kindness you performed for the simple reason that it just felt good, right. Deeds that you may have done to help out a family member, a friend, a stranger. Times when you really felt too busy or overwhelmed with your own life but managed to find it in yourself to help anyway.

Now, for just a minute, close your eyes so you can see the shelves on the right. I imagine they look fairly scarce compared to the ones on the left; but what they lack in quantity, they can make up for it with quality.

Let's continue to add more to the right side. Let's put all the good deeds you did to strangers. Things you did just because you felt extra generous that day. Deeds that no one else saw, but you did it anyway just because it felt right. How's that section looking now? There are so many ways to touch the lives of people we simply can't imagine. How about just expressing a kind word to a stranger? Maybe a compliment or even a simple conversation that might have made their day. How about the last time you just looked a stranger in the eyes and smiled a big sincere smile?

Now we get to look at the best part of the warehouse. You have looked at your past learning experiences on the shelves to your left, the good deeds on the right. Those are the shelves of your life events, the ones that show how you have represented God. Now look straight ahead, those shelves that are right in front of you. They are empty, but in a beautiful and magnificent way. These are the shelves of your future—the place where you will be able to take all the negative learned behaviors on the left shelves and turn them into beautiful new enlightenment that can now be placed on the shelves on the right.

As the shelves on the right begin to fill up, they will bleed over into these middle shelves. When our present and future good deeds become our new learned behavior, they will begin to influence the shelves on the left. Once the shelves on the right bleed over into these middle shelves, they will fill until they buckle, and we experience God like never before.

Let's continue on this journey and learn different ways to fill the right shelves. Let's begin our journey of becoming "One with God."

To love another person is to see the Face of God.

—Victor Hugo

2

LET'S GET THIS PARTY STARTED

This is my Commandment, that you
Love one another as I have Loved you.

—John 15:12

God loves the sinner as much as the saint, the takers as much as the givers, and the losers as much as the winners. His love is incomprehensible, unfathomable to us. Yet He has commissioned us to try and love like He does and to make that love all inclusive. Now, let's get to that party.

This party will be unlike any you have ever attended. You will not need to bring anything. Everything we need will already be there. Dress is whatever you deem it to be, but to be honest, most of the other guests would probably feel more comfortable if we least wear something. This is the biggest party that has ever been thrown; in fact, there is not a venue large enough to house it, so it will be held outdoors.

Let's talk more about who is coming to this party. Wow. There are so many people there, everywhere. Hundreds of famous people. Now I am not a name-dropper, but we are talking A-listers. All your favorite actors, actresses, athletes, artists, and musicians are there. You are running with the big dogs. Come on and let your imagination run wild. You can invite anyone you want; there is plenty of room. This is the event of the century, so everyone should be there: doctors, lawyers, bakers, carpenters, mechanics, hairdressers and so on. You are smack-dab in the middle of it. How are you feeling? Excited? Nervous? Scared? Intimidated? In your comfort zone or out of it?

Continue to picture more people there. All your family, friends, and neighbors are there. Your old classmates are there. Well, keep looking around because there are still hundreds and hundreds more there. There are the homeless people and those that are sick and dealing with diseases. Imagine for a moment how this event is making you feel. Did you see the group of burned victims off away from everyone because of the way people stare? Keep looking, and you'll see those that are addicted to drugs. You'll see the ones that are the drug dealers that sold them. How about that group of kids picking on and bullying that one little guy? Like I said before, everyone is there. How are you feeling? Take a minute to imagine all these people in the same area. There are so very many people with very different personalities, social status, different races and religions.

As you can see, as I said earlier, this event is big. Now, I'd like you to take a step back and allow yourself to simply be an observer, seeing every person there. In your mind, imagine every one of those we discussed earlier, even those that seem to be literally hiding in the corners. Here comes the interesting twist to the party: I'd like you to close your eyes and count to ten. Try and allow yourself to see them all. Keeping your eyes closed as you imagine them all.

When you open your eyes, what you will experience is something slightly different. I need you to completely follow the next instructions. Hope you are ready.

It's time to open your eyes. This time there is only one small difference than what we saw before. When you open your eyes, imagine that every single guest at the party is *you*! That's right, you are the actors and the athletes; you are the doctors and lawyers. You are every single person at the party. You are the homeless, the drug dealers, and the addicts.

I really need you to continue to imagine this party, the exact party you were at in the beginning, only now you are the only guest but in every single body. You really need to put yourself in each person's shoes. You need to imagine what you think they might feel. Try, if you will, to feel their happiness or their sadness or even their physical pain. Take a moment to put yourself in their shoes.

I'd really like you to try and imagine, if only for a moment, what their emotional pain might look and feel like and the heaviness or coldness they might carry every day. Experience through your mind how the homeless must feel. Imagine just one cold night with nothing but a cardboard box and tattered jacket to keep you warm or the days that spike over one hundred degrees and there isn't much relief from the heat. How about worrying about where your next meal will come from, the scars you carry inside that you must be reminded of each time you pass a storefront window. How about the actor who draws attention 24/7 even when he just wants to be normal? What is normal anyways? Being able to afford any meal you want but not being able to do it without interference or is scraping your change together and eating a dollar burger in anonymity? Would these two be envious of each other in some strange way?

The concept of walking in someone else's shoes is difficult and takes great effort. This part of the chapter is not to be scanned or hurried through. It is to be reflective and digested, but I'd like you to continue. Spend time with each one, see what they see, and feel what they feel. Good luck!

I want you to remember our burn victim whom we had trouble seeing because he was off hiding. What if you knew that he received those scars because he selflessly entered a burning apartment to save a family he didn't even know, never hesitating or thinking how that one instant of courage would change who he is and how he looks forever, but knowing that he would do it all over again if called upon? Does that help the scars fade, allow the face to be more palpable?

What about our drug addict that hovers over in the corner, desperately needing a fix just to survive the day? What is his story? Did he lose his entire family when they were hit by a drunk driver? Did he turn to alcohol then pills then to needles, looking for something—anything—that would numb him to the reality of his loss? What about the homeless man who has suffered from mental illness his entire life? His family tired of "babysitting," and the state didn't have the funds to help him? There are the sick and terminally ill who are just praying for a little bit of normalcy in their day. Hopefully, you are beginning to understand exactly what we are trying to achieve here.

If you are truly allowing yourself to feel what each guest at the party is feeling, I would imagine that you might have experienced a wide range of emotions: sadness, empathy, depression, hope, empowerment, and a little exhausted. Would it be possible for us to walk in the shoes of every person we encounter daily? Absolutely not. To experience so very many emotions at the same time is simply a task that most can't do day in and day out. People, imperfect as we are, can be exhausting. Yet He manages to love each one of us the same. There is nothing we can do to make God love us more, nor is there anything we can do to make Him love us less. His love never falters or leaves us. This is the way He wants us to love one another. God sent us his son, to do exactly that, and He came to teach us to do the same.

It is what you do with this knowledge, from here on out, that will help you understand this part of the journey. Only then have you taken your first step into your journey of becoming "One with God." For you see, this is how God feels every day. Every minute of every day, He witnesses the party here on earth, seeing Himself in each of us. He hurts when we hurt and rejoices when we are happy. Kind of mind-blowing, right?

Welcome to God's view.

Give love and unconditional acceptance to those you encounter, and notice what happens.

—Wayne Dyer

3

NATURE

In the Beginning, God created
the Heavens and the Earth.

—Genesis 1:1

As our journey continues, perhaps it is time to slow down a tad, get
back to the basics, to the gifts that God gave us in the beginning:
nature. It's incredible and amazing that He drew in and let out a single breath, and life began. One breath, and He created all the beauty
that takes ours away. I know that He is always near, always knocking
at the door, but sometimes it takes me getting back to nature for me
to feel near Him.

Man, in his desire to connect cities and through hard work, created roads and highways that provide us with passages to the places
we want to go; however, God had much bigger plans. He gave us
paths and trails so we could go to the places we need to go, to the
places that allow us to see and touch and smell the majesty, beauty,
and serenity of the world He created for us. And, my dear friends,
what a world it is! He created a little something for everyone. There
are oceans and seas that crawl right up to sandy beaches, mountains
that stretch to touch the heavens and rivers cutting through them,

jungles and rainforests that cleanse the air that we breathe. There are even desserts, if that's your type of thing. On the days that logistics and time prevent us from making the trek to the places we need to see, He gave us the gift of imagination. If you are really good at it, you can travel anywhere you want in a matter of seconds. It really is a great way to travel as the costs are nil and there isn't any jet lag. So, let's take a little trip together in our minds. Let's give it a shot. Why not? Right.

If you will humor me for just a few seconds, I believe the trip we take will be worth the few minutes it takes to get there and back; that's assuming you do want to come back once you get there. All you will need is to find a quiet place void of interruptions and distractions. Close your eyes, prepare for landing, and enjoy the trip as we head off to the beach. You can choose a beach where you have been before and may hold special memories, or you can choose a beach that is new to you. It really doesn't matter because it's the beach, for goodness's sake. It's going to be great! The beach chairs and ice chest have been unloaded, and sunscreen has been applied, so let's roll.

Our footprints have been etched in the warm sand and have left a path that ends where the water meets the land. Wow! From the shore, the ocean seems endless, infinite, and the only thing that keeps it from being so is our knowledge that the waters we see can touch another beach halfway around the world where someone else is sharing your exact thoughts in a different language.

We watch as a wave folds over and pounds the water below it, churning and turning up the sand. It will be followed by another, then another and yet another. The rhythmic dance and sound of those waves will entertain us for our entire stay, and they will be there for the next person to enjoy and for our sons and daughters and their sons and daughters. The sounds are therapeutic, and if we let them, they can rock us to sleep.

We squint to see ships in the distance, the harbor, and imagine where have they been, where are they going, who are the people who work on them? The ocean bears so many gifts and reminds us how small we are. We are sedated by the sounds of the waves breaking and strolling up to the shore. The sun kisses our bodies, and the heat from its rays can only be tempered by the ocean breeze or a dip into the waters before us.

As you stretch out your legs from your beach chair, can you feel the millions of grains of sand between your toes as you massage your feet with them? Can you hear the breeze rustle the beach reeds behind you, creating a musical that is only interrupted by the sounds of the seagulls begging for food from someone throwing them chips? Can you feel the sand as it attaches itself to your moistened body? Do you smell the ocean and taste the salt in the air? If you can close your eyes and see, feel, touch, hear, and taste the beach, then count your blessings: it is a gift.

Now, let's rinse off, regroup, and take another trip. We will choose the mountains as God created the beaches and the mountains and everything in between. How I do love the mountains. The goal is to get to the top, and it won't always be easy. It takes planning, hard work, and stamina. At times, each and every step seems painful, yet each one gets you closer to the summit, and each one provides a new and unique view of the world that lies beneath it. If we are fortunate, we will have a friend to lend a hand or take a hand to make the climb easier, more enjoyable.

Here the air is fresher, thinner. The trees provide shelter for the animals that dwell in its hollows. One never knows what he or she may have the privilege of seeing, being a part of during the ascent. A spotted fawn, a red fox, rabbits, and squirrels are following their daily routine, and we are but spectators. In the vastness of the mountains, who knows, you may touch a piece of the earth that has never been touched before and maybe never again. It is yours!

From the beach, the clouds look eons away, untouchable; but the hike up the mountain has brought them closer, and if we are sincerely lucky, we may even walk right through one on our way to the top. What an amazing, giving world. The mountains give us crisp, clean air, vision, hope, perspective, and clarity. They bring us nearer to God, and they are well worth the climb, the effort.

God gave us this beautiful place we call Earth, home. If we are still and learn how to listen, we can hear the sounds of the sun coming up; a new day, a new beginning, another chance to get it right. If you have ever experienced a sunrise in the mountains or a sunset from the beach, surely you will think, *Wow! God had a really good day when he came up with this idea!* You would be right in believing so.

God created the heavens and the earth in the beginning. It is as if He wanted to get everything just right when five days later, He created man and woman. He put everything in place for mankind to prosper, to grow, to find peace and joy, and yet He gave us choice to do with it as we see fit. With those choices, we have a responsibility, a duty to protect it and keep it the way God gave it to us. That duty is another step, another level in our journey of being one with Him—oneness.

If we are to please Him, then we are to care for the gifts which He has entrusted us with. Nature was here long before we were, and it will be long after we are gone. We are basically on a loaner program. Many years ago, my father taught me that when you borrow something, you always return it how you got it or even better than when you received it. God is my Father, and I believe He has the same message. It is up to every one of us to do our part to leave this world the way we got it, or better for the generations that follow. Shoot, it's even okay to do more than your part (you know, to offset the slackers). We should toil in the gardens of the world with joyous hearts not because we have to do it or we feel guilty not to do it but because they have been gifted to us; they are of God.

I sincerely believe today that God is disappointed in us and the direction we are going. Why wouldn't He be? Yet He continues to love us unconditionally and to forgive us for our failures when we ask for it. This is another gift, another lesson from Him. It is how each one of us should feel about everyone else. How rejuvenating to be able to love unfailingly and forgive mercifully. If people don't know any better or just don't care how they threat nature, then we need to step up. Don't get mad or judge, just be more like God.

Always leave places better than you found them. We cannot let other people's behaviors and biases change who we are and what is right and expected. See, it is not our job to fix others but to inspire others by our actions. Words can encourage, but it is the efforts people will remember. Now let's get out there and inspire others to return this land to the way we got it or even better. This will allow us to continue on our journey of becoming "One with God."

We practice letting go. And in
the process, we find peace.

—Leo Babauta

4

THE STAIRCASE

I can do all things through Christ
who strengthens me.

—Philippians 4:13

Imagine, if you will, a beautiful staircase. I'd like you to imagine what your own set might look like. There are so very many different styles of stairs. I am using the winding staircase in my own journey because I think they are unique and beautiful. For, you see, this is how God sees each of us.

The way I'd like to explain this portion of our journey is to begin by saying that each one of our journeys are as unique as you and I. No two experiences will be the same, and there is no right or wrong way to begin. As a matter of fact, most of our journeys have already begun.

The purpose of the "staircase" is the simple fact that it heads in a direction to someplace higher. We all know that they can also go down as well. I'd like you to envision your own staircase and where you see it ending. Remember, we are on a spiritual journey together, learning to become godlike or "One with God." For me, I'd like to imagine the top of my stairs where God resides or sits while I'm still living here on earth.

When looking at this situation, imagine that each stair is part of our own ascension into becoming a higher self. Every step you take to the next level must be done with so much compassion and heart. Each step will require a new level of your love and patience. Are you thinking all this sounds easy enough? Again let me remind you, your journey is yours and yours alone. You cannot consider this a competition. It is not about trying to get there first or too fast. It's simply about getting there.

There might not be an award handed out to the first few that arrive to self-love, but the rewards waiting at the end of each step along the way will be such a personal achievement and its own satisfying reward. My own personal reward looks a little like God looking down at me with an approving nod and reassuring smile. That reward makes me excited to plow on and continue in an upward direction to my next step.

What does a step in this process look like? Each step should represent a release, a part of our past behavior that hasn't been so godlike. It might look like resentment or jealously. It could also have a heavy heart about someone we felt has done us wrong in our life. It looks like anger, disappointment, or even fear. Other areas we can all work on are cattiness, arrogance, and judgments toward those we either dislike, despise, or possibly don't even know. I know I personally have quite a few areas I have been, and continue to, work on.

As hard as the things above are to change and work on, these learned behaviors, the harder steps become those that require forgiveness to others and, even more so, forgiving ourselves. Letting go of our own discrepancies and locked up anger and fear is much harder and more challenging. Just remember, this is a process and not a race; but the sooner you learn to let the small things go and the "not so small things" that you can't control, the more in tune with your higher self you will become and the better you will begin to feel overall. After all, isn't that the goal? To feel complete within is to feel complete with God.

I wanted to remind you that there is no perfect way to achieve all this glory without a few steps back. Remember, stairs do go in both directions. If you slip, it's not about taking a step back but learning to catch yourself quickly so that you can get right back on track.

The goal for each of us is up, toward God. Up and forward is good, where down or backward is simply not advancing in a forward direction. Accepting our own past mistakes and forgiving ourselves is possibly the hardest part of the process. Always remember, God's love is already within us. He has already forgiven us. Just know He is with you every step you take, and He will always be by your side, offering His unconditional love, the kind He wants all of us to feel toward others.

Every step on our staircase is a step toward new acknowledgments and acceptance toward others and ourselves. We need to continue to move upward toward the greater good of our existence.

Another way to look at the staircase: it's simply a journey to a greater "self-love" so that we can fully learn to love others as ourselves. We are all worthy of a greater love, a higher love, the highest love.

Once we have established a true self-love, the way God sees us as a temple for Him, then and only then can we learn to accept and love all others as they are, an extension of us. This part of our journey is a self-realization and self-growth that will truly pull us closer toward our goal of being "One with God."

There are no limits on what you can
achieve with your life, except the
limits you accept in your mind.

—Brian Tracy

5

PHYSICAL STATE OF MIND

Do you not know that you are the temple of
God and that the spirit of God dwells in you?

—1 Corinthians 3:16

Being of a physical healthy state is as important as being of a healthy emotional and spiritual state. They really do go hand in hand. That is not to say that you need a six-pack or to be one of the best bodies on the beach. It isn't as important about the outcome of the physical body as much as the way it makes you feel. We were all given these bodies to use and live in while we are living out our lives.

It doesn't take a rocket scientist to see that everyone is given very different bodies. Some need not do much and simply look fantastic all the time while others struggle with gaining too much weight, and others can't seem to put on weight. There are the athletes and dancers who have the physical bodies working in their favor, but if you have ever been in their shoes, you know all the hard work that goes into maintaining the physical self to stay able to compete.

I don't want this to become about trying to develop the greatest body; I want it to become about maintaining the healthiest body—a body that feels better when you get up in the morning, a body where the aches and pains are much more minimal to the days of getting up and getting moving because that is what makes you feel better.

Let's talk a little about how to make small changes toward a physical state that will continue to make us feel not only better, but whole again. As we grow older, our bodies tend to become a product of what we have created. For instance, if we work all day at a desk only to come home and relax in front of the TV, our bodies begin to ache at even the smallest activities.

Now if we were to come home and go for a small one-mile walk before settling into our easy chair, our bodies will not only thank us, but we might even feel energized enough to be somewhat productive around our home. It's very interesting that when we do physical activity, our bodies tend to want more. Don't be surprised if that one-mile walk quickly becomes a two-mile walk. With all we have going on in our systems, to get to a place our bodies are craving activity is the goal/dream for a much healthier physical body.

Stretching is another very important activity for our bodies. When you stretch your limbs and torso, again you are preventing yourself from years of aches and pains in your joints and back. Just the smallest amount of time on a daily basis will make such a big difference that after being consistent for three or four weeks, I'm inclined to believe you will not even want to stop because of the way it will make you feel.

A moving body is a healthy body. Believe it or not, if you struggle with your weight like I have most of my life, you will see the weight start coming off, and that is just another way you will begin to feel better as a whole. It's not the eating that is keeping the fat cells around but a lack of body movement. Our bodies store fat because they are protective over us and think we need to save for a rainy day, so to speak; but the more activity we do, the more our bodies will begin to trust us to make the right decisions.

Just a quick biology reminder that over 60 percent of our bodies are made of water. So it makes sense that we should drink a large amount of water each day to replenish the fluids we lose. I know most of you have heard that drinking water is good for you. I can't stress this enough, but water is *great* for you. You should allow your body to take in as many ounces a day as the pounds you weigh. So if you are a man who weighs 180 pounds, you should be drinking at least a gallon of water a day. Sounds like a lot of water, I know, but our bodies need it.

Many times I sit down to eat a meal, and I do not stop until I feel physically ill. It tastes so darn good that I just keep eating and enjoying until I don't. A great way to prevent this is to drink eight to sixteen ounces of water prior to eating. This will allow you to fill up faster and eat half as much as you may have, leaving enough for lunch tomorrow. Boom! Didn't overeat and saved money on lunch. I know it sounds crazy and may not taste as good, but drinking water will keep you full, replenish your daily fluids, help you lose weight and feel better in general. Plus, it's free when straight from the tap.

As in the concept of being baptized in water to cleanse our sins, water is used to flush out the impurities that attack our organs and immune systems. When our immune systems are not running on all cylinders, we tend to catch every flu, stomach bug, and cold around. Imagine if we could help our immune systems fight a better fight simply by adding more water to our diet. Game changer in my opinion. So if you are inclined to make a step in the right direction, consider drinking more water. I understand that it is somewhat, okay, really tasteless; but for the best results, we should learn to appreciate that boring, tasteless, colorless game changer.

We've talked a little about exercise (or simply keeping our bodies moving), and we have talked about the importance of water. Another area that I'd like to touch on is the food that we put in our bodies. There are many studies out there about what foods are healthy and what foods are not. Let's face it, we all seem to crave the foods we know are not as good for us.

My personal weakness is hot wings. Oh my goodness, I would eat them every day if I could, but I realize that wouldn't be that smart. I only allow myself to indulge every so often. Along with that, learning it's not about the chicken but the flavoring, I like to replace chicken with carrots or celery. That way I get my fix, and I continue a path that is more suitable for a healthy outcome. I'm not here to tell you what or what not to eat; that is strictly your choice. What I am asking is that you listen to your body. The answers to what we should eat lie within each one of us. If something immediately causes heartburn or indigestion, probably not the best for us. We all need to be aware of how different foods affect our bodies. Now I can't fix you anymore that you can fix me; but by listening to our bodies, perhaps we can begin to throw around the word *moderation*. I believe most things are acceptable if done in moderation.

The last area that I would like to touch base on is the toughest for many to control: sleep. Your sleep pattern as well as the amount of sleep you get is extremely important to your overall physical health. Everyone is different on the amount of sleep they need, but we are all the same when we are talking about the quality of sleep we get. There are those of us that can power nap for twenty minutes and seem extremely rested and ready to go; while others, after taking a twenty-minute nap, then only want it to be extended to that two-hour nap. Again, since we are all so different, it's important to listen to your own body for the right answers. Our bodies are very different, so we need to learn and get to know our own body and what it needs.

One thing I'd like to share with you, while we are talking sleep, are a few things that I believe help create a more complete and restful sleep. First, if you are one who enjoys action movies, remember to stop watching anything intense or violent at least an hour before going to sleep. Our minds continue to work and race even as we fall asleep. Turn off that tube, and cozy up with a good book to let your mind fall into a calmer state.

After you read, get in your comfortable position. Just concentrate on your breathing for a few minutes. Take in a deep breath, hold for a moment, then release out of your mouth. With each inhale, think of an event from the day; then with the exhale, let it go and give it to God. When we worry, it also keeps us from a good sleep. When we release our events of the day, we are trusting God to let Him carry our burdens and to believe in Him.

I am now at a point that I trust God to help me with any problems. You will be amazed how freeing it is to turn your wounded heart and troubled mind over to Him. I still do my part to fix any problems I can, but I let God do all the heavy lifting. I just do His will. Being able to let go of worries will allow you to have a higher quality of sleep. Turning everything over to Him is better than taking any medications. If you don't believe me, then believe Him. We can train our minds to relax and accept a sleep routine that, with practice, will work like a charm. That is our hope, at least. Sleep is essential to good health.

By incorporating some of these small things into our daily routine, we can make a significant difference in the way we feel physically. To feel good spiritually is amazing, but it is not enough if we want to live our best life. Our bodies need to become the temples that God wants them to be. You see, God wants our very best selves so that we can go out and meet the goals that will put us on a path to a much better place. When we are fully complete within ourselves, we can help others find the person they are destined to be, therefore going out into the world to be godlike or "One with God."

Be kind whenever possible. It is always possible.

—The Dalai Lama

6

OLD DOGS AND CHILDREN

Who teaches us more than the beast of the earth
and makes us wiser than the birds of heaven?

—Job 35:11

Let's examine an element of our existence that is innocent and vulnerable, a part that counts on us for guidance, protection, and direction—those that have a purity about them until they become tainted and changed by the world's ideas and behaviors and prejudices.

In 1972, Tom T. Hall wrote a song about old dogs and children. It's a catchy tune with a subtle rhythm and beat, so much so that if you're not careful, you will focus on the tune instead of the lyrics—but don't. The music is what lures you in, but the words, well, the words can change your life. The refrain simply says, "Old dogs care about you even when you make mistakes, and God bless the little children while they're still too young to hate." Can you imagine a world, a life where adults were more like old dogs and children?

Babies and children are some of our most valuable resources. They are born innocent and free of bias and hate and every other behavior that is learned. They absorb the lessons that those around them teach and model. The behavior that every parent or older sibling portrays is the behavior that will become the norm for that child.

We have the power and opportunity to mold our children in the likeness of God. I realize that at some point in time, the world will get its hands and influences on that same child, but what he or she learns from those around them will be what is at their core, their base, and their rock. There is an old saying that goes something like this: "People may forget what you say, but they will never forget what you do." Children are always watching us, so we need to be aware of how their actions will begin to reflect ours over time—the good, the bad, and the ugly.

Let's talk about the animals we choose to bring into our homes and the ones that just show up at our doorsteps; you know, the ones that show up with those needy eyes as if they have been searching for us their entire lives. When we bring these little balls of fur and goodness into our homes, we need to only give them what they are here to give us. They just want to love and be loved, just like God wants us to love and be loved.

Children and pets have a way of melting away the toughest exteriors we have until they reach our hearts. Imagine a big burly man with a hard exterior. If you were to follow him into his home, you might witness him instantly approached by his big old pit bull. The two have several moments of pure unconditional love between them. They both just understand the unspoken language that it is okay to be exactly who they are while giving their purest love to each other. If you are not receiving the same love from your four-legged pets, maybe you have not quite let them feel your love as our burly friend above has.

Cats and dogs, while quite different, still provide the same level of love. Cats are curious and cautious, slow and sneaky, but very playful and engaging. They are more the introverted energies, and they tend to check out the scene without much ado. Dogs, on the other hand, will give every single bit of themselves if they feel safe while doing it. We can learn volumes about love and loyalty from our pets if we only take the time to watch and learn.

Can you imagine a world where people are as kind to each other as they are to dogs and cats? Have you ever seen someone walking their dog or, possible, you walking your dog and someone stops to ask if they can pet her? Why is it that others want to connect with your dog but don't show interest in connecting with you? It's as simple as the person asking to pet your dog knows with their whole heart that there will be absolutely no judgment from your dog.

Dogs and cats are here to be beautiful energies that remind us that unconditional love is attainable within each of us. Even the dogs and cats that have been harmed or abused in their lives can forgive and learn to trust again. When they do, it's almost as if they had never been abused in the first place. Imagine if mankind could learn to do the same. Maybe even becoming a much stronger version of ourselves that not only forgive but become the person that behaves the opposite of those that have hurt us. Then we can become a voice for others who might have more difficulty letting go of hurt.

Pets are here to be bundles of everything that is good and right about love without restraints and is potentially in each of us. We talk about training our animals, but maybe God put them here to train us. Maybe we tend to overthink love and compassion and forgiveness. Maybe our pets are right in as much as those traits should be simple and not overthought.

I believe that every type of animal has important lessons for each of us here on our journey to our oneness with God. It is amazing that such diverse animal kingdoms learn how to coexist. Wild animals don't kill for pleasure or hate or for revenge; they simply kill to survive and attack when it is time to feed. There is a hierarchy on the chain of power. Everyone knows their given roles in the "circle of life," and it is just the way it is. Animals will not kill their own species unless they feel so extremely threatened by another. There is simply a respect that they give each other.

Again, imagine just for a moment if our human species behaved the same, not wanting harm for each other. Trusting in God so much that we need not question everything and everyone we don't understand. We may not always agree with one another or understand one another, but that should not keep us from loving one another. We can learn to accept situations we can't change or people we don't understand simply because it's all part of our circle of life, and there is plenty of room here for everyone that seems different.

God put every different type of animal here on our planet because we need everyone for the role they play in our universe. We don't have to understand their purpose, but that doesn't make them any less important. Next time, before you kill any living creature, ask yourself, "Does my family or do I feel threatened by this?" Chances are that you do not. Maybe that creature picked the wrong time to cross your path. We are not always responsible nor do we always expect everything that is going to cross our path as we make our journey through life. How we react to the creatures that cross our path is always up to us, and we need to hold ourselves accountable for all our actions, not just the good ones.

Let's go back to where we started—the love of our domestic pets. We bring these fur babies into our lives because of the way they make us feel about ourselves. We love them the way we do because they make us feel loved just the way we are. We don't have to try and impress them. They already see us for who we truly are; they see our inner selves. They are happy to just sit by our sides and love us the way we are.

Imagine a world where we were able to feel that at our job or in our own families. God loves us much in the same way as our pets do: unconditionally. Can you imagine a world where we receive and give that kind of love to others? Maybe it's time we learn some lessons from our old dogs and children. Oh, I'm not saying this will be a walk in the dog park, but any and all extra effort toward seeing others' good inner self before judging the "not so good" parts of them is what will continue to keep us on our journeys of becoming godlike or our "Oneness with God" selves.

When you judge another, you do not
define them, you define yourself.

—Wayne Dyer

7

JUDGMENTS

Judge not, and you shall not be judged.
Condemn not, and you shall not be
condemned. Forgive, and you will be forgiven.

—Luke 6:37

People always have and always will have an opinion on just about everything, some strong and some indifferent, some that become convictions over time. The problem with opinions is that most of the time, they lead us to making snap judgments that end up being incorrect and hurtful. It doesn't matter if we verbalize our judgments, share them with others, or keep them neatly tucked away in the corners of our minds. The fact that our first response of others is to judge them should be concerning for all of us.

I know that I have made quick judgments in the past that once I had all the facts or got to know the person, I was embarrassed that I ever felt that way. Keeping our judgments to ourselves will certainly help society as a whole, but it will not allow you to complete this journey if we do not delve into the root of our judgments and prejudices. Most of the opinions we make are based on preconceived notions that we have learned and observed since birth. You remember those learned behaviors that sit boldly on the left side of the warehouse. Certainly, making judgments doesn't originate from our hearts. So, how in the world do we turn those negative learned behaviors around?

A great place to start is with the little bundle of joys that join our families every day. We all know and we have all heard that babies are not born with hate or prejudices. They are incredibly innocent little beings who in their formative years will soak in everything the people around them say and do. In order for them to learn tolerance for anyone and everyone who is "different," we need to step up and exhibit those characteristics.

Parents are the greatest influence on small children and can have the most impact on how they view the world. Will there be other influences that could potentially undo or change what we as parents instill? Of course, but it is up to us to lay that solid foundation on which to build. I believe that each generation carries with its certain beliefs and ideas. I believe that the times in which people grew up has played a big part in the way they believe—the fifties, sixties, seventies, eighties, etc. We were taught by society at first, and as society corrected themselves, our parents were not ready for the changes.

So those prejudices continued to flow through our families. Each generation seems to get closer to a more open acceptance of others. This journey we are embarking on, the main goal is to become the very best version of ourself. It is to grow stronger from the inside which will take all the inner drive we can muster and may be one of the harder parts of the journey to attain.

There is nothing simple about the task we are about to encounter, but I can promise you that the rewards will be unlike anything you could have ever imagined. You will have a lighter burden and a happier existence. The benefits of learning to love and accept all people will manifest itself into the most beautiful life imaginable.

The first step to learning to love all people is to learn how to forgive ourselves. We cannot accept others if we cannot accept ourselves. Carry every hurt and scar, every transgression as a medal of honor and a reminder that you are striving to become whole. To become complete, we must begin to accept and love others regardless of our differences because when it comes right down to it, people are more alike than they are different.

I understand that there are times that seems it's important to voice an opinion or defend an idea. There are certain values and ideals that we hold dear and will defend. Differences of opinion are a reality; however, the way we approach those differences will be the defining moment on how much we have grown. Our message is heard much louder when we talk softer. We must listen to one another with open ears, minds, and hearts. Regardless of our different backgrounds or beliefs, two souls connecting on a level of understanding and grounded from the heart will have a greater impact than any of our differences. We need to learn to live and stay in the moment.

It is important to know that becoming "one with God" is not about religion but, rather, about building a personal relationship with God. Religion is great, but your own personal relationship with God is the journey we are on. One should never use their religion as a weapon to rip apart any other person and their beliefs. God did not create religion. God created a mantra for all humans to adhere to. He created the Golden rule: "Do unto others that you would have done unto you."

Jesus came to earth as an example of what each of us could be. He did not want glory or praise for what He did. He did not want to be idealized but simply loved and respected just as He loved and respected others. He did not gravitate to those with wealth and power; instead, He went to those in need of a kind and loving energy that He had to offer. He surrounded Himself with the weak, the downhearted, the lost, and the broken. He searched out those in need of the great love he had to give.

If you are old enough, you might remember the WWJD phase. "What would Jesus do" was a phrase that people wore on bracelets, t-shirts, and other items. Everyone wore it proudly. Well, I believe we should bring it back with just a small adjustment. Instead of it saying "What would Jesus do," I believe it should say "Do what Jesus did"—DWJD. Can you imagine a world, if even for a day, if everyone DWJD? Could you imagine it for a week? How about a year? What? It would be like we had thousands of Jesuses here to make life better for others and, of course, ourselves.

It might take a while before we are feeling thousands and thousands of Jesus-like people, but it can begin immediately for someone else through you. You have the same exact qualities as Jesus did. You just must learn how to tap into that part of yourself then go out and share it with the world.

All beings are equal in God's eyes. No species is more important than the others. No religion is more superior than the others. There isn't anything we can do to make Him love us more or anything we can do to make Him love us less. To believe that any one man ranks higher in God's eyes because of beliefs or social status is the whole purpose of this process. He loves us unconditionally, for He created us. That means that we need to try and be our best version of us for Him. Don't place everything that you have ever been taught above your own gut instinct, for that gut instinct is God's direct line to you.

The fact that we judge another human being is one of God's least favorite things we do. See, God knows the daily challenges we each face. He knows our hearts and our thoughts. He knows the heart of the judged and of the judge. Regardless of your upbringing or your current prejudices, it's extremely important to teach yourself to let go of certain parts of what you have been taught, what you have learned. Learn to look at everyone as though they are an extension of you. It's an extremely challenging task, but I know that with His guidance, you are up for it. Just remember, when things seem to be the hardest and we are at our lowest, God is always there with us every step of the way.

When we learn to love and accept others just as they are and not as we wish they were, it will surely be one of the most rewarding moments we experience. For, you see, when we worry less about how others are and more about how we react or respond to them, we make ourselves accountable and, once again, take another step closer to our "Oneness with God."

Act as if what you do makes
a difference. It Does.

—William James

8

PAYING IT FORWARD

By this all will know that you are my
disciples, if you have Love for one another.

—John 13:35

The use of the term *godlike* or the phase "one with God" isn't an expectation of perfection. We are simply trying to achieve a perfect love we put back into ourselves, others, and the universe. God knows each of our personalities and sees Himself in each one of us. He wants to see Himself shine through each of us and embrace others.

A society is responsible for all the ugly as well as all the good it sees in the universe. For it is us as a society that can change things, one kind act at a time repeated over and over until it's the only action we have or see.

When we begin to look at others as extensions of our own existence, beauty begins to flow and kindness spreads. We are all aware of the "pay it forward" theory. A single act of kindness daily can feed your soul as much or more than it feeds the soul of the one who received the kindness. Some days you might do two acts or four acts or more. Think of the trickle effect of days with more good deeds. When someone thanks you, simply say, "When you get the chance, pay it forward." Then just like that, a love chain has begun, and I like to think the repercussions will create the world that each of us really wants to see. It isn't going to happen overnight, but the very best things in life usually take time and nurturing.

In your mind, imagine if you did two kind acts a day, those two then did two more acts to two people. Those four people did their two acts to two more people. Right there, your two acts. Have turned into thirty acts of kindness, spreading the idea that love and only love can transform this world to become the world we all long to see. You see, your acts of kindness not only help a person out and bring joy to their day, they also help the person giving the kind act feel more connected to a society, therefore wanting to add to the overall outcome of a more united world.

Of all the steps in this book, this is probably one of the easier ones to achieve without too much effort. I believe most people have more kindness than negative in them, therefore most likely have done small acts of kindness throughout their lives. All we are looking to do here is make it a part of your daily routine. When you think about it, to help out another or do something kind won't take more than a couple of minutes out of your day, and it will make the day turn out so much better for you simply because you will feel very pleased with yourself. Let's face it, work is smoother, life is better when we are in a good place in our hearts.

Let's talk about the big old warehouse for a few minutes. Remember how very full our left side of the shelves were? Remember how "not so full" our right side was? Well, just imagine, if you will, what those right shelves would look like in a year if following the simple task of doing a couple of kind acts a day. Suddenly those right shelves don't seem so hard to fill.

I can also assure you that every act of kindness you do will begin to reshape your own life into becoming one that you could have only dreamed of. Once God knows that the direct line between you and Him is open and ready, everything you have ever wanted will begin to manifest in your own life. God has always been here for us. He has offered us guardian angels, archangels, and earth angels. The only catch to receiving these higher-power gifts is to simply ask.

God gave us free will as a humankind, so God told the angels, "You must not interfere unless you are asked." So, whether you want to believe it or not, you have every tool you could ever imagine at your fingertips. God and his Angels will be on call 24/7, but they insist that your heart be full of love and purity before they can help you manifest your dreams. When your dreams become less selfish and more about the overall good, the possibilities are endless.

I'd like to share my story about how I came to write this book. I began the practice of asking the archangels and my guardian angels to help me make a difference daily, to put me in situations that I felt drawn to a stranger or friend who needed some form of love or acceptance. More and more I found myself in the right place just when someone needed another friendly face. The more I asked, the more I received. Anyway, years later, I wanted to learn more about how these angels, with God's direction, could continue to improve my life. So I began studying their strengths and what their purposes were. Lo and behold, it is not necessary to know them all by name. Simply knowing that there is a greater energy ready to help you at each turn in your life becomes empowering.

I have never been much of a reader and certainly never imagined writing anything. So as I began to fully understand the concept of our guides (angels) almost overnight, I would wake up between 3:15 and 4:30 am with so much information I felt pulled to get up and write it all down. Now I'm not exactly your morning person. As I always had dreams, there was something much different about these wake-up calls. My head would be swimming in information I just needed to jot down. So I'd write it on my pad only to crawl back into bed for a little more sleep. Usually when their juices were flowing, or rather they realized I was letting mine flow, they would wake me again only to write a little more. Once I woke up for the day, it might be a couple of hours before I would go back and read what I wrote. I could not believe it. These certainly were not my words—not my doing, but somehow it was. The next time I woke, it was the outline of the book. Boldly gave me the title and even how many steps to partake in it.

The purpose of me sharing this story with you is the fact that I started off asking for selfless things—to be the person someone randomly needs—and it became more about trusting that God has my best interest at heart and only wants good for me. We are all a reflection of what we put into the world. Let me say that once more: We are all a reflection of what we put into the world. As long as you try to put your best forward (and trust me, that is not always the easiest) and you keep trying, your life will turn around, and you will be provided with everything you need or want as long as it's for the greater good. You are never alone, for you see, God has so many guardians, angels, and spirit guides working along with him to assure we are all loved and taken care of.

Once you learn to incorporate the small acts of kindness to where it becomes part of your daily routine, I believe you will notice that your life will begin to take on a whole new direction—one that you will be happier, more fulfilled, and more at peace. For, you see, this is another step in your journey of becoming godlike or "One with God."

Spread love everywhere you go Let no one
ever come to you without leaving happier.

—Mother Teresa

9

LET YOUR GOD SHINE THROUGH

And be kind to one another,
tenderhearted, forgiving one another,
even as God in Christ forgave you.

—Ephesians 4:32

We have had quite the journey thus far. I'm hopeful that with all the places we have been in our minds, you feel anxious to begin to have the life that only you could have imagined and hoped for. Each of our journeys begins and ends with God. As I have mentioned, we are each on our very own journey to becoming a soul that not only we are proud of, but can 100 percent, without doubt, know that God is proud of.

If you could, for just a moment, think about all the things that you believe that you would be happier with—possible a new car, a bigger house, more money. Now imagine for a moment that you can have all this and more. When we realize that our own actions can put us in control of ourselves and no one else, we can be in control of our own life and, therefore, our own destiny.

To say that all this sounds easy is quite the stretch. It will take a lot of commitment, but the rewards are priceless. Once we begin to look at ourselves as a being created by God for God, then we can begin to let our guards down and become the person that we were created to be. We each have different stories that brought us to the place where we are now. What we chose to do with the rest of our lives is up to us, and once we realize that we already have all the tools we need to get us to our desired place, we become empowered.

God says, "Go out and take care of others, and I will take care of you." For, you see, when you help others in need, they are seeing God through you. God exists in each of us, and it is our job to let Him shine through. It doesn't matter to this point what you have done in your life. It matters from here on out how you behave if you want the truest, happiest self-possible. When you accept the challenge of stepping out of your comfort zone into the unknown, the rewards and outcome could be amazing. We can do anything we chose to do.

We should always push young people to follow their dreams. For when our dreams get pushed down so far because we allowed society to convince us we couldn't achieve them, part of us also dies a little. Let's breathe new life into these dreams and create a world that everything is possible. We all exist in the society that we have contributed to. We have become what we see and what we are told we see. Let's turn our own reality into the world we want to be a part of.

Remember, when taking on these challenges of trying to achieve a higher self, we must be prepared to give our power to God, then and only then will our lives begin to shape the future which few can only dream of but all are capable of. It will take lots of hard work and it probably won't happen overnight. God is in you, and He is ready to help you bloom into the beautiful soul that He already sees.

In the previous chapters, we talked about several ways to be kind to others and ourselves, to begin to see everyone out there as an extension of us, without judgment but with a love that God would feel for them, then we can truly know the purest love that God has for each of us.

One thing I'd like to say is when you finish this book and go back to your life that was perfectly fine, know that God loves you as much, if not more than ever. His love is truly so pure that He already knows how each person will respond to this book. I was blessed with insight to be able to write this book. Does it mean that I have all the answers? Of course not. I must remind myself not to get frustrated or impatient often. Remember, we are still humans but with the spirit of God living within us.

People need only be around some people, and they feel a loving presence there. A shared smile can connect two souls, and that is God working through them. Allow your soul to actually feel another's soul. It is one of the most satisfying experiences imaginable. When we accept others as ourselves, whether we understand them or not, that is God shining through us. Once others see and feel that kind of love and acceptance, then you will know you are "One with God."

Sometimes the smallest step in
the right direction ends up being
the biggest step in your life.

—Steve Maraboli

10

CONNECTING THE PIECES

Believe me, that I am in the Father, and the
Father in me. Most assuredly, I say to you,
he who believes in Me, the works that I do
he will do also; and greater works then these
he will do, because I go to My Father.

—1 John 14:11–12

This is what Jesus said to his followers. He believed that He was no different than you and me. He came to be an example to us. He showed us how we are supposed to treat each other, yet we fail in so many ways. Hopefully, this book has helped close the gap between God and us just a tad, that it serves as a reminder of how we should live and love others.

One of the first things we need to do is to declutter our lives and minds. Basically, let go of anything, and yes, anyone that pulls us away from where we are headed on this spiritual journey. We can continue to love the people that hold us back, but we will never move on until we learn to let go.

The next step is to learn to see others as a part of ourselves, as we did at the party. We need to practice the act and art of stepping out of our shoes and into the shoes of others, to feel what they are feeling, before we pass judgment. We must have compassion and empathy for other people, to try to understand their journey and the pains and hurts that may have been a part of it. Continue to do this as often as possible, and it is always possible.

We want to remember to look at our earth through the eyes of a healer. Pick up a piece of trash instead of just stepping over it. You need not be in one of the most beautiful places to contribute to the beauty of our earth. Hopefully others will see you doing good, and who knows, they might just join in. Remember that change can begin with but a single step. Make that step.

These other steps will become so much easier when you have begun the work on the staircase in your own life letting go of past pains and learning to avoid future pain, forgiving others who have done you wrong but also letting go of your own insecurities and built-up resentments. Like I said, this is one of the more challenging steps but with the most rewards waiting on the other side. You will begin to see your world become brighter with each passing day, therefore making the next steps on your journey somewhat easier.

Take back your health, own it, reward your body and mind by taking care of it. Begin a routine where you let your body lead you rather than you leading it. Listen to it. When we start listening to our bodies, it will let us know the right things to eat and drink. Drink more water especially before eating. Let your body become a little full from the water before sitting down to dinner. Remember to stretch and move a little more each day, keeping those limbs young and nimble. Let's not forget to work on that sleep schedule. Learn what is the healthiest amount of sleep for you, keeping in mind you could be one of those getting too much sleep. That will keep you in a groggy cloud all day.

Give those fur babies exactly what they are here to give you—love, love, and more love. Take note how you feel when your pet is sitting next to you and just loving you for exactly who you are. Then let's not hide that love away from the world.

If you find yourself making an instant judgment on someone passing by, catch yourself and make yourself think of at least two things you like about the same person, maybe even share one with them. It will make their day, and it offered a gentle reminder to be less judging in an already harsh world. Let's not be one of the ones making it a harsher world. We want to be one that begins healing the world.

How fun is the concept of "paying it forward"? Think about being in line for a coffee, and the guy in front of you buys yours. That's something you go straight to the office and can't wait to share. Made a great start to your day. As good as that feels, it can actually feel just as good, if not better, to be the giver instead of the receiver. Be the person that makes someone else go to work and share what an amazing start to their day they just had. It feels good to be the one doing randomly nice things. Let's create a world where these things don't have to be so random.

Finally, letting your God shine through will take little to no effort once you have put these other steps into action. It will have begun a change in yourself that not only God will notice but, I guarantee, you will too. You will look at the person in the mirror and begin to see exactly who God sees—your innermost beautiful self. When you see that person, everything in life will begin to transform into the world you could have only imagined.

The way we respond or react to other people's actions is very important to our growth. We should focus on a much more positive attitude during our journey into a higher self. The more we deny the outer negative forces, the easier we can achieve our goals.

Instead of thinking it's your job to save others by bringing them into your religion, possibly the concept of saving others comes from a place of pure acceptance. Maybe showing love and acceptance is the way to help others find God, letting them know that God's love is unconditional and that the greatest love exists right here on earth. No one religion will take you to the spiritual finish line. Truth is all religions can help with the journey, but it is only one's innermost self that can bring it all home. Looking within one's self is truly the only way to a "Oneness with God." Looking within is how you fill God's destiny of your best self.

Like we said earlier, we are responsible for all the ugly or beauty we see in the universe. It is our own truth we take from every situation. The truth is there is much more beauty in the world when we see it through an awakened soul. To awaken spiritually is to view everything we have ever believed from a different perspective—God's perspective.

Experience a life, in your head, where we are all souls instead of physical beings. The only thing you can see on someone else is their energy (whether good or bad). You can't see looks or style, can't speak or hear; you can only see what they feel and how they respond to you and others. Of course, that is all they can see in you as well. There are no promises to be better or I meant that with good intentions, only raw behavior. Try and become the soul that others look toward for inspiration and leadership. Remember, to inspire or lead others rarely needs words. Let your behavior become everything that lights others' way. Let your behavior become godlike, and in the end you will truly be "One with God."

Be somebody who makes Everybody
feel like a Somebody.

—Robby Novak

ABOUT THE AUTHOR

K. R. Snoek is a Texan, born and raised from the southeast part of Texas. She currently resides in the Houston area with her two small dogs. She felt very pulled by her spirit guides to begin her writing career. She has three grown boys whom she is very proud of because of their beautiful hearts and desires to make this world a better place for all others. Although writing wasn't originally part of her life journey, she is fully embracing all the opportunities that lie ahead in her future. With much excitement and anticipation, she looks forward to wherever this journey takes her.